HE STARTED IT!

HE STARTED IT!

My Twitter War with Trump

Danny Zuker

with Paul Slansky

Griffith Moon

ISBN: 978-0-9998452-8-8
LOC: 2018952754

Book Design by Sara Martinez
Cover illustration by Scott Shaw
Paul Slansky's Twitter portrait by Lulu White

Printed in the United States of America
First Printing, 2018
Published by Griffith Moon
Santa Monica, California
www.GriffithMoon.com

"When I look at myself in the first grade and I look at myself now, I'm basically the same. The temperament is not that different."

— Donald J. Trump

This book is for

All of you who not only vote
but get everyone you can to vote

The press, the champions of the people
(except for you, and you know who you are,
who actually do spread "Fake News")

All of the hundreds if not thousands of
women who have been the victims of
Donald Trump's sexual "misconduct"

Preface

by Paul Slansky

In Danny Boyle's 2002 film *28 Days Later*, a Cambridge research lab has been conducting experiments on chimpanzees caged in darkness. The only light comes from 360 degrees of screens showing nothing but beatings, riots, fires, torture – a round-the-clock barrage of the most violent videos imaginable.

Enter an animal liberation group. A panicked scientist comes in and warns them not to release the chimps, who are infected with a highly contagious virus. This warning is, of course, ignored, and the first ape freed bites the activist, and let's just say carnage ensues. Cut to four weeks later, and London is populated by zombie-like creatures infected with the "rage virus," intent on infecting everyone else.

We are currently living through a version of *28 Days Later*. In this analogy, Newt Gingrich, Rush Limbaugh, Sean Hannity and the rest of their depraved ilk comprise the group that's spent two decades exalting ignorance, demeaning truth and preaching bigotry, seeding and feeding the rage virus. Donald Trump is the ape that sunk its teeth into America, infecting its population with the filth that spews from his appropriately sphincter-shaped mouth, liberating the haters to let loose and connecting the rest of us with feelings we never thought ourselves capable of, all the while making the public discourse safe for incivility, indecency, and insanity. Safe for *inhumanity*.

* * * * *

The world was blissfully unaware of Donald Trump until October 16th, 1973, when, at the age of 27, he made his debut as a public figure on the front page of *The New York Times* in an article headlined, "Major Landlord Accused of Antiblack Bias in City." His first public utterance, in response to charges of violating the Fair Housing Act of 1968, was, "They are absolutely ridiculous. We never have discriminated, and we never would." Enter lying.

The tawdry escapades that propelled him to tabloid fame over the course of the ensuing decades have been exhaustively chronicled in dozens of books and articles and need not be recounted here. But for all the millions if not billions of words that have been written about him, none convey his boorish infantilism more mercilessly than those "best" ones he puts into his tweets.

Trump's Twitter career began innocuously enough on May 4th, 2009, with a boilerplate staff-written plug for his upcoming appearance on David Letterman's show to promote *Celebrity Apprentice.* Eight days later, his fifth tweet expanded his repertoire to include quoting himself: "'My persona will never be that of a wallflower – I'd rather build walls than cling to them'—Donald J. Trump". Already with the walls.

For more than two years his sporadic tweets were offensive only to those repelled by braggadocio (and the improper usage of "there," "their" and "they're"). Then, on July 7th, 2011, he let fly his first attack tweet:

If only @Obama was as focused on balancing the budget as he is on weakening Israel's borders then America would be on the path to solvency.

At this point, the tsunami began.

The now omnipresent theme of self-pity was introduced a month later, in one of the seven tweets he issued on August 3rd: "Morning Joe Panel is stealing many of my statements and ideas to better America without giving credit – the story of my life!" (*The story of his life!* Poor little lamb! And only 28 Likes.) "Losers" first appeared six days later, applied to the folks at Standard and Poor's.

But it was Obama, who had eviscerated him to his seething face at the 2011 White House Correspondents Dinner, who he targeted relentlessly with tweets that are now retroactively hilarious:

@BarackObama played golf yesterday. Now he heads to a 10 day vacation in Martha's Vineyard. Nice work ethic.

Why did @BarackObama and his family travel separately to Martha's Vineyard? They love to extravagantly spend on the taxpayers' dime.

@BarackObama gave 1% of his income to charity from 2000 through 2004 http://t.co/C3rtWcoT I guess he only likes spending our money.

and on

Michelle Obama's weekend ski trip to Aspen makes it 16 times that Obamas have gone on vacation in 3 years. Insensitive. @BarackObama

and on

When I was 18, people called me Donald Trump. When he was 18, @BarackObama was Barry Soweto. Weird.

and on

.@BarackObama was caught telling Russian PM @MedvedevRussiaE that he can be more 'flexible' in his second term. Russia thinks he's weak.

and on

Obama's war on women has lead to the biggest decline in female employment in 40 years. 4 more years??

And, of course, on.

His next regular target was MSNBC's Lawrence O'Donnell ("I heard, because his show is unwatchable, that @Lawrence has made many false statements last night about me. Maybe I should sue him?"), with Rosie O'Donnell following soon after ("I am so glad @Rosie got fired by @Oprah. Rosie is a bully and it's always nice to see bullies go down!")

By December of 2011, the two O'Donnells had joined Obama as Trump's Twitter triptych. Another milestone that month: the "Sad!" tag debuted in a tweet about Fox News's token Democrat, Bob Beckel: "He ruins the brand: @Robertgbeckel doesn't belong on @FoxNews. As CM for Mondale in '84, you lost 49 states. Sad!"

He was just getting started. In 2012 he tweeted more than 3,500 times – an average of almost ten tweets a day. A few highlights:

> Almost all reporters falsely report that I had a 'bad time' at last year's White House Correspondents' Dinner. The opposite. I had a great time and thought the President did a good job-- and was very funny.

> The electoral college is a disaster for a democracy.

> It makes me feel so good to hit 'sleazebags' back -- much better than seeing a psychiatrist (which I never have!)

Still, for all his pugnacity, he managed to tweet for four years before getting into his first sustained Twitter war, which brings us – finally – to this book.

The 13th season of *Celebrity Apprentice* started on Sunday, March 3rd, 2013. Hundreds of tweets over the next eight weeks were dedicated to promoting the show and boasting about its alleged ratings success. On April 29th – eight days after @realDonaldTrump tweeted, "I know some of you may think

I'm tough and harsh but actually I'm a very compassionate person (with a very high IQ) with strong common sense" – his 7,795th tweet provoked a response from *Modern Family* producer Danny Zuker.

What follows is a three-month-long exchange between Danny and the future President, who was then merely the clownish host of a reality show and the leader of the deranged birther movement – a national buffoon but not yet the global menace he has tragically and unequivocally proven to be.

Tens of thousands of tweets have been posted since this five-year-old exchange – all of them available for masochists at http://www.trumptwitterarchive.com/archive – but you have here the first sustained digital display of petulant puerility by the man who now holds the fate of the world in his undersized hands.

By his tweets ye shall know him. But then, of course, you already do.

IT TRULY WAS A COMEDY WRITER'S DREAM. Donald J. Trump, failing reality star and America's biggest assclown, actually engaged with me on Twitter.

It was the spring of 2013 and it wasn't a great time for our porcine prince. His God-awful reality show was dying in the ratings. His political ambitions were laughed at by the GOP. He actually scheduled his own summit for the candidates running to unseat Obama and every single candidate snubbed him. He made a film for the 2012 Republican convention that was so awful even they wouldn't show it. So great was his need for attention that he led the birther movement, a movement so extreme and ridiculous that only the most racist fringe elements of the Republican party embraced it. In short, to use one of his "best words," he was a loser.

And surprisingly stupid. As you read through our three-month-long exchange, it's impossible to see Trump as anything other than a world-class simpleton. During the Twitter war, I was lauded for taking this bully down, but really, nothing could have been easier. It felt like being cheered for dunking on a toddler. I mean this sincerely: any of my friends could have easily KO'd the imbecile. He just picked me. But I'll gladly accept the accolades.

And man, oh man, were there accolades. While pretty much everything you can tweet will stir up that vocal minority of the easily offended, the love I got for beating on the brat was nearly universal. Republicans, Democrats, Northerners, Southerners – they all heaped on the praise. It seemed the one thing this country could agree upon was that Donald J. Trump was a ridiculous little pig man. And then, two short years later, the grammatically challenged hate tweets began to fly my way. Enough Americans were conned by this cretin to hurtle him to an historic victory. Historic in that he lost the popular vote by three million and was aided by Russian interference, but still. Seriously? President?

I couldn't believe it. I still can't. Every morning I wake up and the first thing I do is ruin my day by remembering that there is a mentally ill maniac in the White House. (Or, a third of the time, at Mar-a-Lago.)

On the first anniversary of the most traumatic election in U.S. history, I was invited to read aloud the entirety of my Twitter war at a fund raiser for Puerto Rico relief. The great Tim Simons from *Veep* had the thankless task of reading Trump's part. The audience both loved it and was horrified by it. I mean, it's funny. Knocking down a pompous ignoramus always is. But the reality that this, as the phrase goes, fucking moron is now the President made it less funny. My dear friend Paul Slansky was in the audience that night and he insisted that we release this as a book and donate all proceeds to causes that Trump's policies are harming. Based on the feedback that night, I knew it was the right thing to do.

It strangely feels like an important document now. All the childish language and the insane logic he used to engage me, he's now using with world leaders. (Not Putin, but nearly everyone else.) Our backs and forths read like some twisted beta test of all that was to come.

Donald Trump is president not because he's changed. He is not just incapable of change but sees no need for it. No, this idiot is the leader of the free world because *we've* changed.

But let's travel back to a simpler time: April 29th, 2013. I'm sitting on my couch scrolling through Twitter, which I'd discovered a few years earlier. Twitter was a great platform for jokes and, since I started my career as a joke writer, it was fun to exercise that muscle again. The main focus of my tweets was my ineptitude as a husband and father. These were the kind of jokes that might have been a little too mean for *Modern Family*, where I've been working these past nine years. Anyway, as I scrolled through that day's feed I saw that Donald Trump had tweeted a (brace yourselves) lie.

I had on occasion called this reality "star" out on his bullshit, particularly the birtherism he was championing. But jokes at a celebrity's expense always felt a little easy. I wasn't above making them but always felt a bit dirty doing it. I rationalized it with Trump because of his stature as one of the more despicable people I've had to share the planet with. But he never tweeted back – until I called him out on his lie. Then the floodgates opened.

What follows is my digital dance with the dipshit.

The Tweets

Donald J. Trump ✔
@realDonaldTrump

Just out - @ApprenticeNBC was in first place in all demos during the 10PM hour in the ratings.

1:40 PM - 29 Apr 2013

18 Retweets **28** Likes

Danny Zuker ✔
@DannyZuker

Cool story. Here's how you really did. RT @realDonaldTrump @ApprenticeNBC was in first place during the 10PM hour.

9:00	FOX	Family Guy	2.5/7
	ABC	Revenge	1.7/4
	CBS	The Good Wife - Season Finale	1.6/4
	NBC	Celebrity Apprentice (9-11PM)	1.5/4

2:02 PM - 29 Apr 2013

155 Retweets **252** Likes

I had tweeted about his racism and his stupidity, but it took exposing his miserable ratings for him to engage. This clearly foreshadowed his going bananas about his inauguration crowd size.

Donald J. Trump ✓
@realDonaldTrump

"Failed show @DannyZuker" I have never heard of you and was told you are a loser- after reading your credits I have no questions about it!

4:32 PM - 29 Apr 2013

69 Retweets **89** Likes

Donald J. Trump ✓
@realDonaldTrump

.@DannyZuker I hear your filmography is "stacked" with failures.

4:33 PM - 29 Apr 2013

29 Retweets **43** Likes

Yes, I worked on *Stacked*. He's not wrong for mocking that.

 **Donald J. Trump** ✔
@realDonaldTrump

"Failed show @DannyZuker" season 1 of
@apprenticenbc had 28 million viewers and
41.5 million watching.....

4:36 PM – 29 Apr 2013

20 Retweets **20** Likes

 **Donald J. Trump** ✔
@realDonaldTrump

... but you only want to talk about 10 years
later when I still win 10PM in all key demos.
@DannyZuker

4:36 PM – 29 Apr 2013

6 Retweets **6** Likes

 **Danny Zuker** ✔
@DannyZuker

Replying to @realDonaldTrump
.@realDonaldTrump @ApprenticeNBC **Although
last night your ratings were lower than CB Radio.**

4:37 PM – 29 Apr 2013

54 Retweets **185** Likes

The idea that he compares ratings from fifteen years ago to
ratings five years ago tells us that, for all of his obsession with
them, he has no idea whatsoever how ratings work. He still
does this. He actually took credit for the Super Bowl and the
Oscars being down in the ratings. Pardon the all caps but EVERY
FUCKING SHOW IS DOWN IN THE RATINGS, AS WE NOW
CONSUME OUR ENTERTAINMENT ON MULTIPLE DEVICES.

Donald J. Trump ✓
@realDonaldTrump

.@DannyZuker **Don't lie,** @ApprenticeNBC
was #1 in all major demos at 10. Do not lie!

5:16 PM – 29 Apr 2013

14 Retweets **18** Likes

Danny Zuker ✓
@DannyZuker

Replying to @realDonaldTrump

.@realDonaldTrump @ApprenticeNBC **The
only way you could be losing rating points
faster is if you inherited them from your
father.**

4:41 PM – 29 Apr 2013

329 Retweets **795** Likes

Sometimes I'm proud of my jokes. This was one of those times.

Donald J. Trump ✓
@realDonaldTrump

.@DannyZuker I'm in front of the camera and behind the camera- just looked at your picture, you'll never be in front of the camera!

5:14 PM – 29 Apr 2013

43 Retweets **34** Likes

Danny Zuker ✓
@DannyZuker

.@realDonaldTrump Yes how could I compete with your beauty.

5:17 PM – 29 Apr 2013

121 Retweets **302** Likes

The fact that this man, who literally – and I AM using this word correctly – looks like a pig that drowned, believes he is the ultimate arbiter of beauty is high on the list of his many delusions.

Donald J. Trump ✓
@realDonaldTrump

"One hit wonder @Danny Zuker", I notice you are not disputing all of the failures that I said you had. Let's talk about it!

5:15 PM – 29 Apr 2013

36 Retweets **29** Likes

Danny Zuker ✓
@DannyZuker

Replying to @realDonaldTrump

.@realDonaldTrump I've had failures. Not lose my inheritance go bankrupt a bunch of times & become a paid race baiting buffoon, But failures.

5:26 PM – 29 Apr 2013

340 Retweets **869** Likes

Little did I know, it would be that very race-baiting buffoonery that would land him in the White House.

Donald J. Trump ✓
@realDonaldTrump

"@DaltonStoltz: @realDonaldTrump 2.1 Mil.
Followers vs. @DannyZuker 189 Thous.
@realDonaldTrump is WINNING!
#GreaterInfluence He has nothing

8:05 PM – 29 Apr 2013

13 Retweets **10** Likes

Danny Zuker ✓
@DannyZuker

.@realDonaldTrump Sorry I missed your last
response. Was watching a Family Guy rerun.
You know like the reruns that beat you each
week! #LOL

8:46 PM – 29 Apr 2013

103 Retweets **333** Likes

I don't want to get in a dick measuring contest with the only guy I'm absolutely positive I could beat. However, he had more than ten times my number of followers and check out who got the most retweets and likes.

Donald J. Trump ✔
@realDonaldTrump

"@PyperProblems: @realDonaldTrump someone needs to fire @DannyZuker !" He will fire himself-a total loser!

9:11 PM – 29 Apr 2013

19 Retweets **15** Likes

Donald J. Trump ✔
@realDonaldTrump

"@jtan_from_ott: @realDonaldTrump would ever have a loser like @dannyzuker on the apprentice? His stupidity could be funny. Interesting!

10:53 PM – 29 Apr 2013

14 Retweets **32** Likes

I have to give it to him: Stupidity can be funny.

Donald J. Trump ✓
@realDonaldTrump

"@kilgorecf: Dang @DannyZuker @realDonaldTrump has been too good." No, too easy-Danny is a dummy!

10:56 PM – 29 Apr 2013

18 Retweets **9** Likes

Danny Zuker ✓
@DannyZuker

.@realDonaldTrump How long does it take to find someone who supports you & not me? I've been scrolling for 10 minutes & haven't found a one!

11:06 PM – 29 Apr 2013

23 Retweets **173** Likes

I mentioned this in my introduction, but it was truly remarkable how little support he was getting.

 **Donald J. Trump** ✔
@realDonaldTrump

"@MasSergio: @realDonaldTrump **that punk's jealous of ya mr. trump** @DannyZuker **is not worth the time of day! He prolly wants media attn-True!**

11:09 PM – 29 Apr 2013

14 Retweets **8** Likes

 **Danny Zuker** ✔
@DannyZuker

.@realDonaldTrump YOU just accused ME of wanting media attention? Okay you win. I will never write anything that funny EVER!

11:12 PM – 29 Apr 2013

92 Retweets **373** Likes

Paul Slansky told me early in Trump's campaign that "every accusation is a confession." Nothing has helped me understand him more. He tells us the Clinton Foundation was pay to play and then makes a fortune using his position to funnel world leaders to his horrible hotels. Obama played too much golf and… well, you get it.

Donald J. Trump ✓
@realDonaldTrump

"@PureManhattan: @DannyZuker @realDonaldTrump Id rather support The Don than some clown. Just saying. Danny, you are a clown." Yes and loser!

11:20 PM – 29 Apr 2013

16 Retweets **13** Likes

Danny Zuker ✓
@DannyZuker

.@realDonaldTrump No offense. I'm just ribbing you on account of you being utterly despicable and a general cancer on society. #Night.

11:39 PM – 29 Apr 2013

280 Retweets **578** Likes

Donald J. Trump ✓
@realDonaldTrump

Replying to @DannyZuker

@DannyZuker **Night loser!**

11:42 PM – 29 Apr 2013

110 Retweets **125** Likes

I have more than a few friends who, when getting off the phone with me, still close with, "Night loser!" So, thanks for that.

Danny Zuker ✓
@DannyZuker

.@realDonaldTrump I owe you an apology. Last week I said your show couldn't be doing any worse. I was wrong. #sorry

Broadcast primetime ratings for Sunday, May 5, 2013:

Time	Net	Show	18-49 Rating	18-49 Share	View Live+ (milli
7:00 PM	FOX	NASCAR Overrun (7-8:30PM)	2.3	7	7
	ABC	America's Funniest Home Videos	1.5	5	5
	CBS	60 Minutes	1.2	4	10
	NBC	The Voice -R (7-9PM)	0.9	3	3
8:00 PM	CBS	The Amazing Race (8-10PM)	2.3	6	8
	ABC	Once Upon A Time	2.2	6	7
8:30 PM	FOX	The Simpsons	1.7	5	4
9:00PM	FOX	Bob's Burgers	2.0	5	4
	ABC	Revenge	1.8	5	6
	NBC	All-Star Celebrity Apprentice (9-11PM)	1.4	4	4
9:30PM	FOX	Family Guy	2.1	5	4
10:00 PM	FOX	American Dad	2.1	6	5
	CBS	The Mentalist	1.7	5	9
	ABC	Red Widow	0.9	2	3

1:41 PM – 6 May 2013

77 Retweets **186** Likes

What separates me from Donald, apart from genus and species, is that I am happy to admit when I'm wrong. Damn, I wish I'd tweeted this!

Donald J. Trump ✔
@realDonaldTrump

It's go time! See you at Trump Tower. I'm giving money away! #FundAnything

12:07 PM – 8 May 2013

94 Retweets **78** Likes

Danny Zuker ✔
@DannyZuker

Replying to @realDonaldTrump

.@realDonaldTrump Have you heard of these #Losers who do charity WITHOUT issuing press releases & making it all about themselves? #LOL

1:27 PM – 8 May 2013

133 Retweets **249** Likes

Let's see what *The Smoking Gun* had to say about his generosity in the article headlined: "Trump: The least charitable billionaire."

http://www.thesmokinggun.com/documents/celebrity/trump-least-charitable-billionaire-109247

 **Donald J. Trump** ✓
@realDonaldTrump

I AM PLEASED TO INFORM YOU THAT
CELEBRITY APPRENTICE HAS BEEN
RENEWED FOR ANOTHER SEASON BY
NBC. SEE YOU AT THE NBC UPFRONTS
TOMORROW.

7:44 PM – 12 May 2013

309 Retweets **360** Likes

 **Danny Zuker** ✓
@DannyZuker

NBC will pick up @realDonaldTrump's
Celebrity Apprentice for another season as
part of the networks strategy to "continue
sucking."

9:18 PM – 12 May 2013

215 Retweets **250** Likes

By the way, at those upfronts no such announcement was made.

Danny Zuker ✔
@DannyZuker

.@realDonaldTrump **hasn't tweeted in almost
24 hours. I do hope something's wrong.**

4:44 PM – 18 May 2013

82 Retweets **212** Likes

My kids can't even believe that there was a time when he could
go twenty-four hours without tweeting.

 **Donald J. Trump** ✓
@realDonaldTrump

.@MELANIATRUMP, @IvankaTrump, @EricTrump, @DonaldTrumpJr & I thank our loyal fans for another great season of @ApprenticeNBC!

2:01 PM – 20 May 2013

36 Retweets **61** Likes

 **Danny Zuker** ✓
@DannyZuker

Take the next 12 minutes & thank them each individually. RT @realDonaldTrump I thank our fans for another great season of Apprentice.

2:47 PM – 20 May 2013

44 Retweets **142** Likes

Not to get too nostalgic but back then, when he tweeted the names Melania, Ivanka, Eric and Don Jr., I didn't feel like vomiting.

Donald J. Trump ✓
@realDonaldTrump

"@danrpriest: @realDonaldTrump **Just out of curiosity, what makes you care so much about what they think?" I study cowards and stupid people**

6:25 PM – 24 May 2013

76 Retweets **86** Likes

Danny Zuker ✓
@DannyZuker

Your house has lots of mirrors?

6:34 PM – 24 May 2013

285 Retweets **465** Likes

I pitched a joke with this punchline on about a half dozen shows I've worked on to no avail. I'm glad it found its perfect home here.

Donald J. Trump ✔
@realDonaldTrump

I was just told by a television pro thay
@DannyZucker is one of the truly dumbest
guys in the business-he's obsessed with T-so
many flops!

6:53 PM – 24 May 2013

43 Retweets **42** Likes

Danny Zuker ✔
@DannyZuker

.@realDonaldTrump I just talked to an un
named human decency pro and he said you
were a narcissistic hateful uninformed ass
clown.

7:12 PM – 24 May 2013

195 Retweets **448** Likes

"So many flops." There really is something so insanely funny
about this slam. Many of my friends would greet me by shaking
their heads and saying, "So many flops." I think no one loved this
as much as Andy Richter, who to this day will randomly write
those three words to me. It's now in my Twitter Bio.

Donald J. Trump ✔
@realDonaldTrump

I never heard of @DannyZucker until his very
dumb and endless tweets started pouring
out of insecure mind-but I have a great deal
for him!

7:02 PM – 24 May 2013

32 Retweets **33** Likes

Donald J. Trump ✔
@realDonaldTrump

@DannyZucker, are you ready for the deal?

7:11 PM – 24 May 2013

6 Retweets **3** Likes

The deal. I knew from the second he proposed it that the best
way to make him crazy would be to never accept his stupid deal
or show any curiosity about it. I was right. Throughout the rest
of our feud he never stopped bringing it up. It was super fun to
watch him melt down because I wouldn't play his game.

Danny Zuker ✓
@DannyZuker

.@realDonaldTrump @dannyzucker It's
@DannyZuker. It's not as easy to remember
because I don't tackily plaster it all over
buildings

7:06 PM – 24 May 2013

75 Retweets **262** Likes

Donald J. Trump ✓
@realDonaldTrump

"@DannyZuker: @realDonaldTrump
@dannyzucker It's @dannyzucker." As I said,
I've never heard of you before!

7:26 PM – 24 May 2013

17 Retweets **38** Likes

Kinda seems like he heard of me, no?

Donald J. Trump ✔
@realDonaldTrump

@DannyZuker, are you ready for the deal?

7:36 PM – 24 May 2013

36 Retweets **27** Likes

Danny Zuker ✔
@DannyZuker

Replying to @realDonaldTrump

.@realDonaldTrump Does the deal involve a birth certificate or do you take me at my word because I'm white?

7:37 PM – 24 May 2013

240 Retweets **744** Likes

Donald J. Trump ✔
@realDonaldTrump

Replying to @DannyZuker

@DannyZuker Another racist remark by you, Danny, are you a racist?

8:30 PM – 24 May 2013

71 Retweets **79** Likes

Every accusation is a confession.

Donald J. Trump ✓
@realDonaldTrump

I know you don't like to hear this @DannyZuker but the biggest nights of The Apprentice were far "bigger" than the biggest nights of Mod Fam

8:05 PM – 24 May 2013

43 Retweets **35** Likes

Danny Zuker ✓
@DannyZuker

Replying to @realDonaldTrump

.@realDonaldTrump Did you put "bigger" in quotes cause U know ratings across the board were higher a decade ago or was that u being a dimwit

8:11 PM – 24 May 2013

38 Retweets **180** Likes

His random use of quotation marks is fascinating. He truly is a very uneducated "man."

Donald J. Trump ✅
@realDonaldTrump

Replying to @DannyZuker

@DannyZuker **Bigger means bigger dummy, you really are stupid, aren't you!**

8:34 PM – 24 May 2013

29 Retweets **38** Likes

Danny Zuker ✅
@DannyZuker

Don't you want to end that tweet with a question mark?

8:39 PM – 24 May 2013

42 Retweets **117** Likes

I generally don't engage trolls on Twitter but when I do I find nothing makes them angrier than when I correct their grammar, spelling or punctuation. Try this at home!

 **Donald J. Trump** ✓
@realDonaldTrump

Replying to @DannyZuker

@DannyZuker Come on Danny, are u afraid of the DEAL (be careful, I'm really good at deals).

8:38 PM – 24 May 2013

29 Retweets **28** Likes

 **Danny Zuker** ✓
@DannyZuker

Replying to @realDonaldTrump

.@realDonaldTrump Is this one of those deals where you figure out a way not to give any money to charity? Those are cool!

8:44 PM – 24 May 2013

65 Retweets **208** Likes

Well, we now know he made one helluva deal with Putin.

Donald J. Trump ✅
@realDonaldTrump

Replying to @DannyZuker

No @DannyZuker , just the opposite, lots of money can go to charity if you have the guts to play the game (deal)!

8:48 PM – 24 May 2013

21 Retweets **14** Likes

Donald J. Trump ✅
@realDonaldTrump

Remember, @dannyzuker , you are not even the real "boss" of Modern Family - no big $$$$$$'s for you!

8:45 PM – 24 May 2013

53 Retweets **49** Likes

I will admit that when he brought *Modern Family* into the fight, I was a little concerned. The show employs hundreds of people, my friends, and I didn't want them dragged into my battle. I talked to the show's creators, Chris Lloyd and Steve Levitan, as well as the cast, and to their credit they gave me the go-ahead to keep on tweeting!

Danny Zuker ✔
@DannyZuker

Replying to @realDonaldTrump

.@realDonaldTrump So your big comeback is "I have more money than you, na na na na na naaaah?" #Classy

8:54 PM – 24 May 2013

56 Retweets **169** Likes

Danny Zuker ✔
@DannyZuker

I want everyone to bask in the pure awfulness of @realDonaldTrump's last tweet about $$$$$. It's genuinely spectacular.

8:58 PM – 24 May 2013

71 Retweets **219** Likes

Andy Richter ✔ @AndyRichter – 24 May 2013
@DannyZuker I've been saying "so many flops" out loud to myself and giggling

4 Retweets **37** Likes

Danny Zuker ✔ @DannyZuker – 24 May 2013
@AndyRichter It's really fun!

2 Retweets **12** Likes

At the time of him boasting about money, he was hundreds of millions of dollars in debt to the foreign banks he was forced to borrow from when American banks cut him off. To be clear, he lost money running a casino. Take that in.

 **Donald J. Trump** ✓
@realDonaldTrump

Replying to @DannyZuker

@DannyZuker @AndyRichter Danny, you're
not having fun, you are getting your ass
kicked - afraid to make the deal?

8:57 PM – 24 May 2013

17 Retweets **16** Likes

 **Donald J. Trump** ✓
@realDonaldTrump

@dannyzuker I hope you pick up a lot of
twitter followers by this so people can see
what a total asshole you are!

9:03 PM – 24 May 2013

243 Retweets **299** Likes

 **Danny Zuker** ✓
@DannyZuker

Replying to @realDonaldTrump
Finally we agree on something!

9:06 PM – 24 May 2013

25 Retweets **112** Likes

The future president called me an asshole. You're damn right I
wear that as a badge of honor.

Danny Zuker ✔
@DannyZuker

.@realDonaldTrump I love how crazy it's making you that I won't play your stupid game.

9:02 PM – 24 May 2013

22 Retweets **126** Likes

Donald J. Trump ✔
@realDonaldTrump

Replying to @DannyZuker

No @DannyZuker it's making you crazy because you don't have the guts to play the game. Come on Danny, you can do it!

9:08 PM – 24 May 2013

24 Retweets **31** Likes

Danny Zuker ✔
@DannyZuker

Replying to @realDonaldTrump

.@realDonaldTrump Is this a game where when we hear about an epidemic of sex assaults in the military we blame it on WOMEN being in the service?

9:11 PM – 24 May 2013

65 Retweets **204** Likes

This is something he'd actually tweeted earlier that month: "26,000 unreported sexual assults [sic] in the military-only 238 convictions. What did these geniuses expect when they put men & women together?"

Donald J. Trump ✔
@realDonaldTrump

@DannyZuker everyone is saying you are being beaten badly at this game but you can turn things around quickly if you go for the deal.

10:13 PM – 24 May 2013

10 Retweets **14** Likes

Danny Zuker ✔
@DannyZuker

Replying to @realDonaldTrump

.@realDonaldTrump Is there an alternate definition for "everyone" that I'm unaware of? Because consensus seems to be I made you my bitch.

10:15 PM – 24 May 2013

148 Retweets **529** Likes

Currently, "everyone" is also apparently saying there was NO COLLUSION!

Donald J. Trump ✓
@realDonaldTrump

"@kosstar: @DannyZuker @realDonaldTrump
Did we ever get the details of the "deal"?
No, Danny doesn't have the guts to play the
game.

10:41 PM – 24 May 2013

9 Retweets **15** Likes

Donald J. Trump ✓
@realDonaldTrump

@DannyZuker is a weak and ineffective guy
with a long string of failed shows who got his
ass kicked last night.He's afraid to make the
wager

10:01 AM – 25 May 2013

7 Retweets **15** Likes

This guy just gets me.

Danny Zuker ✓
@DannyZuker

@AndyRichter I have to be honest. I think
I'm starting not to like the guy.

2:16 AM – 25 May 2013

38 Likes

Donald J. Trump ✓
@realDonaldTrump

"@DannyZuker: @AndyRichter I have to be
honest. I think I'm starting not to like the
guy." Actually Danny, you would like me very
much!

10:54 AM – 25 May 2013

7 Retweets **12** Likes

His need to be liked is huge. Not huge enough to actually be
likeable but still. I have no doubt that, were I to extend an olive
branch and start complimenting him, I could talk my way into a
cabinet position.

Donald J. Trump ✔
@realDonaldTrump

If @DannyZuker competed against me and.won (which not too many people do), he could win millions of $'s for himself or his charity!

10:20 AM – 25 May 2013

17 Retweets **36** Likes

Danny Zuker ✔
@DannyZuker

.@realDonaldTrump I'll never respond to your asinine bet. Too much fun imagining u stomping around like the troll u are. Trumpelstiltskin!

1:35PM – 25 May 2013

84 Retweets **299** Likes

I was also super proud of calling him Trumpelstiltskin until Paul Slansky called him TrumpelTHINskin. Damn you, Paul.

Donald J. Trump ✔
@realDonaldTrump

"@DannyZuker: .@realDonaldTrump I'll never respond to your asinine bet. You're gutless Danny, and you don't even know what the bet is-loser!

5:56 PM – 25 May 2013

15 Retweets **20** Likes

Danny Zuker ✔
@DannyZuker

Replying to @realDonaldTrump

.@realDonaldTrump Hey since I metaphorically took off your gravity ravaged nut sack yesterday you should take MY bet. You in? Good!

5:59 PM – 25 May 2013

17 Retweets **78** Likes

Who has the best words?

Danny Zuker ✓
@DannyZuker

Here's the bet: Take whatever money you were planning on dangling in front of me & then donate it to Oklahoma relief and then that's it.

6:00 PM – 25 May 2013

68 Retweets **352** Likes

Danny Zuker ✓
@DannyZuker

.@realDonaldTrump I heard Bill Gates actually donates millions to worthy causes without making self aggrandizing idiotic bets. What a loser!

6:05PM – 25 May 2013

149 Retweets **319** Likes

My intuition told me that he was less than pleased to be reminded that there were actual billionaires out there.

Donald J. Trump ✓
@realDonaldTrump

"@CaptainApathyUK: Enjoying reading @DannyZuker knocking the shit out of @realDonaldTrump." Sorry hater, he's getting his ass kicked!

6:34PM – 25 May 2013

40 Retweets **36** Likes

Donald J. Trump ✓
@realDonaldTrump

"@JeffBirotweets: Thoroughly enjoyed watching @realDonaldTrump and @DannyZuker twitter fight. At least Danny has the better hair. He's bald!

6:46 PM – 25 May 2013

7 Retweets **5** Likes

Danny Zuker ✓
@DannyZuker

This may not be your best line of attack.

7:04 PM – 25 May 2013

16 Retweets **79** Likes

I found it curious that he thought it furthered his cause to retweet people who were clearly Team Zuker. Perhaps he's not the brilliant strategist he fancies himself to be. But seriously, what an idiot!

 **Donald J. Trump** ✓
@realDonaldTrump

@DannyZuker **on your best day you can't come close to beating me, I'll kick our ass every time-take the bet Danny (check with M.F. boss).**

7:04 PM – 25 May 2013

29 Retweets **28** Likes

 **Danny Zuker** ✓
@DannyZuker

.@realDonaldTrump **"I'm kicking your ass, wait come back here!"**

6:41 PM – 25 May 2013

45 Retweets **178** Likes

There hasn't been a day in his presidency that hasn't evoked Monty Python's limbless Black Knight.

Donald J. Trump ✔
@realDonaldTrump

"@MikeMcCabeSad: @realDonaldTrump @DannyZuker the fact that you keep tweeting at him is showing why you lost" True, Danny is a known loser!

7:36 PM – 25 May 2013

22 Retweets **23** Likes

Donald J. Trump ✔
@realDonaldTrump

"@djbtv: I hope you folks are following @DannyZuker this weekend as he dismantles @realDonaldTrump." Friend of Danny sorry, he died!

8:12 PM – 25 May 2013

13 Retweets **3** Likes

At least now he's learned to retweet like-minded people such as white supremacists, neo-Nazis and Kanye.

Danny Zuker ✓
@DannyZuker

OK gotta go @realDonaldTrump! I have a busy night of NOT railroading the wrong people in the Central Park wilding case for self promotion!

8:26 PM – 25 May 2013

32 Retweets **83** Likes

Donald J. Trump ✓
@realDonaldTrump

See, dummy Danny Zuker, who I never heard until this, started something that he couldn't finish-gutless and unwilling to take my bet!

9:07 PM – 25 May 2013

40 Retweets **32** Likes

Danny Zuker ✓
@DannyZuker

Replying to @realDonaldTrump

.@realDonaldTrump **Stay down! Stay down!**

9:22 PM – 25 May 2013

13 Retweets **68** Likes

I actually heard from two of the Central Park Five shortly after this. Turned out they were rooting for me. Honestly, it was pretty moving to get those messages.

Donald J. Trump ✓
@realDonaldTrump

"@Iamgrizzly1974: @realDonaldTrump
Furthermore, as we continue to send our
assets to foreigners we will become a 3rd
world country.Must stop.

4:50 PM – 27 May 2013

70 Retweets **38** Likes

Danny Zuker ✓
@DannyZuker

.@realDonaldTrump Thank you for taking
such a brave stand on foreign-- wait what's
this...?

11:36 PM – 27 May 2013

317 Retweets **482** Likes

One day I opened my laptop and saw that I had an email from
Jimmy Kimmel and his wife Molly McNearney. The subject line
was simply, "Do with these what you will..." Upon opening it I saw
that Jimmy and Molly were staying at Trump Soho and had taken
pictures of all the products in the room that were made in China.
Trump provided me many opportunities to use these amazing pics.

Donald J. Trump ✔
@realDonaldTrump

Bringing true luxury to the Windy City,
@TrumpChicago soars 92 levels over the
Chicago River bit.ly/12iDqHu

3:06 PM – 29 May 2013

18 Retweets **16** Likes

Danny Zuker ✔
@DannyZuker

RT @realDonaldTrump Bringing true luxury
to the Windy City,

3:11 PM – 29 May 2013

64 Retweets **138** Likes

I have genuinely tried to avoid making hair jokes. How does the
saying go? "People in bald houses..."? However, as much as I'd like
to be Trump's number one enemy, that title will forever belong
to the wind.

 **Donald J. Trump** ✔
@realDonaldTrump

China has done great under Obama.
Increased private US holdings by 500%.
Hacks our military & R&D. Robs us blind
daily.#timetogettough

1:20 PM – 30 May 2013

414 Retweets **139** Likes

 **Danny Zuker** ✔
@DannyZuker

.@realDonaldTrump You have always led by
example when it comes to China and--
what? Not again!

2:38 PM – 30 May 2013

148 Retweets **288** Likes

I have a file on my computer titled "Trump China" and there are
at least eighty pictures.

Donald J. Trump ✔
@realDonaldTrump

Pres. Obama is meeting with China's Pres. this week politi.co/15ygs2s He will get zero deliverables. China laughs at us.

Obama apt to talk softly with China
He's unlikely to get tough on cyber-snooping when he meets with his Chinese counterpart this week.
politico.com

4:52 PM – 3 Jun 2013

87 Retweets **34** Likes

Danny Zuker ✔
@DannyZuker

@realDonaldTrump Well sir China isn't laughing at you because you always tell them to go to-- hello?!

5:56 PM – 3 Jun 2013

48 Retweets **110** Likes

Today, the whole world is laughing at us. Even the Germans, and they are a tough laugh.

Donald J. Trump ✔
@realDonaldTrump

Remember Trump ties & shirts @Macys for Fathers Day--your father will love you even more!

4:11 PM – 5 Jun 2013

48 Retweets **14** Likes

Danny Zuker ✔
@DannyZuker

MT "@realDonaldTrump Remember Trump ties for Fathers Day." Well surely these must be made in the U.S--what?!

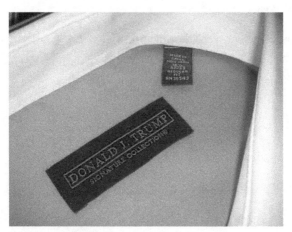

6:22 PM – 5 Jun 2013

123 Retweets **135** Likes

"Your father will love you even more." It's almost SAD.

Donald J. Trump ✔
@realDonaldTrump

"Inspiration exists, but it must find you
working." -- Pablo Picasso

10:49 AM – 6 Jun 2013

489 Retweets **220** Likes

Danny Zuker ✔
@DannyZuker

You've been tweeting all morning.

1:56 PM – 6 Jun 2013

37 Retweets **108** Likes

He has literally spent a third of his presidency on vacation. We
have never had a less industrious president.

Donald J. Trump ✓
@realDonaldTrump

I hope everybody goes to Macy's today to get Donald J. Trump shirts, ties, suits and cufflinks – they are really beautiful at low price.

3:57 AM – 7 Jun 2013

136 Retweets **86** Likes

Danny Zuker ✓
@DannyZuker

.@realDonaldTrump You've always been tough on China, sir. Particularly the children who make your shitty clothes.

1:07 PM – 12 Jun 2013

1,114 Retweets **1,042** Likes

When I'm sad I like to think about how much money he lost by blowing his Macy's deal. But at least he got that wall, #LOL.

Donald J. Trump ✔
@realDonaldTrump

.@DannyZuker Danny – Let your bosses on Modern Family lend you money to play the game. Show courage!

3:13 PM – 12 Jun 2013

39 Retweets **27** Likes

Donald J. Trump ✔
@realDonaldTrump

.@DannyZuker Danny--You're a total loser!

4:26 PM – 12 Jun 2013

154 Retweets **194** Likes

Still with the deal!

 **Danny Zuker** ✓
@DannyZuker

.@realDonaldTrump Your insults need work.
Here's one I've been working on: "Every
picture you post of yourself is a dick pic."
See?

4:28 PM – 12 Jun 2013

243 Retweets **481** Likes

 **Donald J. Trump** ✓
@realDonaldTrump

I can't resist hitting lightweight @DannyZuker
verbally when he starts up because he is
just.so pathetic and easy (stupid)!

4:54 PM – 12 Jun 2013

79 Retweets **44** Likes

 **Danny Zuker** ✓
@DannyZuker

Replying to @realDonaldTrump

.@realDonaldTrump It is adorable that you
think you're winning this. Bless that area on
your body where a heart should be!

4:59 PM – 12 Jun 2013

93 Retweets **328** Likes

This was a preview of the kind of detachment from reality that
would allow him to say, "No President in history has accomplished
more in their first year than me."

Danny Zuker ✔
@DannyZuker

.@realDonaldTrump Since you're unable to manufacture decent comebacks maybe you could outsource the job to China. #LOL #Trumpelstiltskin

5:04 PM – 12 Jun 2013

328 Retweets **679** Likes

Donald J. Trump ✔
@realDonaldTrump

Lightweight @DannyZuker is too stupid to see that China (and others) is destroying the U.S. economically and our leaders are helpless! SAD.

10:25 PM – 12 Jun 2013

112 Retweets **65** Likes

Danny Zuker ✔
@DannyZuker

.@realDonaldTrump I'm def too stupid to see how manufacturing your shitty clothes in China while you bloviate about them isn't hypocritical.

10:32 PM – 12 Jun 2013

215 Retweets **414** Likes

I might also be proud of the outsourcing joke. Do I sound like Trump?

Donald J. Trump ✓
@realDonaldTrump

Just tried watching Modern Family - written by a moron, really boring. Writer has the mind of a very dumb and backward child. Sorry Danny!

10:46 PM – 12 Jun 2013

1,188 Retweets **1,529** Likes

Danny Zuker ✓
@DannyZuker

Replying to @realDonaldTrump

.@realDonaldTrump Doesn't like the show I work on but then we've never tested well with the racist, hypocritical, multiple bankruptcy demo.

10:58 PM – 12 Jun 2013

442 Retweets **696** Likes

"Backward child?" #EveryAccusationIsAConfession

Donald J. Trump ✔
@realDonaldTrump

"@Leigh26Heather: @realDonaldTrump WHO
ON EARTH IS DANNY ZUKER????!!!! A
lightweight moron who only gets attention by
attacking Trump.

11:01 PM – 12 Jun 2013

41 Retweets **27** Likes

Danny Zuker ✔
@DannyZuker

Clearly the one thing @realDonaldTrump
DIDN'T inherit from his daddy was a
thesaurus. #Loser #Dummy #Lightweight

11:06 PM – 12 Jun 2013

135 Retweets **300** Likes

I don't know about "the best," but he definitely has the
fewest words.

Danny Zuker ✓
@DannyZuker

.@realDonaldTrump "Happy Birthday, Boss!"

2:10 PM – 14 Jun 2013

468 Retweets **687** Likes

To this day, I take a perverse pleasure in sending him birthday greetings from his sweatshops.

Donald J. Trump ✓
@realDonaldTrump

"@hellocory: Oh my god the twitter fight between @dannyzuck and @realDonaldTrump" There is no fight with @DannyZuker, he is a nobody!

9:39 PM – 15 Jun 2013

20 Retweets **23** Likes

Donald J. Trump ✓
@realDonaldTrump

"@dooobieashtray: @realDonaldTrump acts childish fighting with @DannyZuker via internet" Wrong, he started it and I finished it-he's nothing

9:49 PM – 15 Jun 2013

53 Retweets **39** Likes

Danny Zuker ✓
@DannyZuker

.@realDonaldTrump For Fathers'Day here's some free advice: When told that you're being childish don't respond with "He started it!"

9:52 PM – 15 Jun 2013

202 Retweets **499** Likes

I mean, how could this not be the title of this book?

Donald J. Trump ✔
@realDonaldTrump

Frankly, for a writer, I don't think
@DannyZuker's stuff is good. In fact, it's
terrible.

5:13 PM – 17 Jun 2013

54 Retweets **41** Likes

Donald J. Trump ✔
@realDonaldTrump

I own @DannyZuker, but he has his friends &
haters & losers tweeting that he beat me. He
can't beat me at anything!

5:13 PM – 17 Jun 2013

60 Retweets **54** Likes

Danny Zuker ✔
@DannyZuker

Only until you go bankrupt again and the
bank takes me. RT @realDonaldTrump I own
@DannyZuker!

9:57 PM – 18 Jun 2013

151 Retweets **330** Likes

I get the argument that a successful business man should run
the country and perhaps one day a successful business man will.
This man *lost money running a casino.*

Danny Zuker ✓
@DannyZuker

.@realDonaldTrump I know you think you destroyed me but I think you've mistaken me for the Scottish countryside or NBC. #StayDown

5:23 PM – 17 Jun 2013

164 Retweets **370** Likes

Donald J. Trump ✓
@realDonaldTrump

I met a Trump Twitter hater last night (well known). As he came near me he nervously said, "Mr. Trump, it is an honor to meet you sir!" Nice

11:45 PM – 18 Jun 2013

508 Retweets **737** Likes

Danny Zuker ✓
@DannyZuker

I said "horror."

11:49 PM – 18 Jun 2013

117 Retweets **269** Likes

Hardly his most egregious sin, but no one over nineteen years old should ever say "hater."

Donald J. Trump ✓
@realDonaldTrump

Snowden is sitting in China and taunting the U.S. He is mocking us as a Country. Great time to place a tax on China trade if not turned over

11:13 AM – 18 Jun 2013

102 Retweets **37** Likes

Danny Zuker ✓
@DannyZuker

.@realDonaldTrump **If only Americans were able to make slippers u could really back up this tough talk on China** 🌀

12:50 PM – 18 Jun 2013

77 Retweets **163** Likes

I'm still stunned that so many American factory workers were able to overlook his rampant and ongoing outsourcing.

Danny Zuker ✔
@DannyZuker

.@realDonaldTrump Uh oh it's starting 2 rain bullshit again! Quick put on this shower cap made in the US of what?

2:31 PM – 20 Jun 2013

108 Retweets **197** Likes

It's kind of amazing he didn't find his third wife in China. But then, he seems to prefer white people.

 **Donald J. Trump** ✔
@realDonaldTrump

@DannyZuker **Loser Danny is obsessed with Trump.**

2:25 PM – 20 Jun 2013

16 Retweets **33** Likes

 **Donald J. Trump** ✔
@realDonaldTrump

"Change is the law of life. And those who look only to the past or present are certain to miss the future." - John F. Kennedy

4:55 PM – 21 Jun 2013

706 Retweets **407** Likes

 **Danny Zuker** ✔
@DannyZuker

"You quoting me is the worst thing to ever happen to me" John F. Kennedy

8:06 PM – 21 Jun 2013

127 Retweets **287** Likes

Where was he getting these quotes? He doesn't read, and Fox was certainly not quoting JFK. Wait, did KFC used to print inspirational quotes on their buckets?

Donald J. Trump ✓
@realDonaldTrump

We are being embarrassed by Russia and China on Snowden (and much more) yet Obama is talking about global warming on Tuesday.

3:26 PM 24 Jun 2013

341 Retweets **157** Likes

Danny Zuker ✓
@DannyZuker

.@realDonaldTrump Don't know about global warming but you know what was created by the Chinese...

5:52 PM – 24 Jun 2013

172 Retweets **263** Likes

It's unclear exactly which articles of clothing are pictured here but what's indisputable is their country of origin.

 **Donald J. Trump** ✓
@realDonaldTrump

We need to worry about the American worker
first!

3:57 PM – 25 Jun 2013

176 Retweets **112** Likes

 **Danny Zuker** ✓
@DannyZuker

So thoughtful of you to not burden them with
the task of making your ties.

4:03 PM – 25 Jun 2013

68 Retweets **191** Likes

Speaking of ties, WTF is it with those insanely long ones he wears
that hang down past his crotch? He clearly pees on them, right?

Donald J. Trump ✓
@realDonaldTrump

What my father really gave me is a good (great) brain, motivation and the benefit of his experience-unlike the haters and losers (lazy!).

8:25 PM – 29 Jun 2013

433 Retweets **395** Likes

Danny Zuker ✓
@DannyZuker

Also $100 million and a 5th grade vocabulary.

9:10 PM – 29 Jun 2013

170 Retweets **272** Likes

Danny Zuker ✓
@DannyZuker

.@realDonaldTrump For the record, I believe the hair on your race baiting, narcissistic, environment raping, uncharitable head is 100% real!

10:02 PM – 29 Jun 2013

128 Retweets **273** Likes

Remember how Einstein and Hawking were always going on about how smart they were? Me neither.

 **Donald J. Trump** ✓
@realDonaldTrump

Via @reason: "Donald Trump: I Can Fix
America"

Donald Trump: I Can Fix America

Donald Trump believes he'd be better suited to tackle some
of America's problems than President Barack Obama – and
that includes repairing strained relations between Moscow and

reason.com

1:02 PM – 1 Jul 2013

33 Retweets **18** Likes

 Danny Zuker ✓
@DannyZuker

You misspelled "fuck."

2:04 PM – 1 Jul 2013

158 Retweets **299** Likes

Kind of an easy joke, but this had been going on for a while. I
was tired.

Donald J. Trump ✓
@realDonaldTrump

"@rodmonium91: @realDonaldTrump Is your war with @DannyZuker over with?" Who is Danny Zuker?

10:55 PM – 23 Jul 2013

6 Retweets **10** Likes

Danny Zuker ✓
@DannyZuker

.@realDonaldTrump Oh dear. How hard did I hit you? Quick how many of your ties made in China am I holding up?

11:42 PM – 23 Jul 2013

51 Retweets **157** Likes

You never can predict someone's last straw but...

Danny Zuker ✔
@DannyZuker

Was it something I said?

7:39 PM – 24 Jul 2013

102 Retweets **645** Likes

...For whatever reason that was his. So, on July 24th, he admitted defeat – or, more accurately, convinced himself he won – and blocked me.

Danny Zuker ✓
@DannyZuker

.@realDonaldTrump I miss us

9:18 PM – 30 Oct 2013

45 Retweets **326** Likes

Donald J. Trump ✓
@realDonaldTrump

"@DannyZuker: .@realDonaldTrump I miss
us. " Danny, I miss you tooooo!

9:38 PM – 30 Oct 2013

20 Retweets **37** Likes

Months after being blocked by him, I jokingly tweeted this and
he responded. I'm telling you, I could be Secretary of State!

Danny Zuker ✔
@DannyZuker

I may disagree with much of what
@realDonaldTrump says, but that doesn't
mean I think he's a terrible person. 4-1-14

1:27 PM – 1 Apr 2014

38 Retweets **240** Likes

Donald J. Trump ✔
@realDonaldTrump

"@DannyZuker: I may disagree with much of
what @realDonaldTrump says, but that
doesn't mean I think he's a terrible person.
Somewhat nice!

1:05 AM – 6 Apr 2014

19 Retweets **45** Likes

So, it had been a year since the feud started and months since he'd blocked me. I'd still tweet at him, but to silence on his end. Then I paid him this fake compliment and he jumped back in. This is the level of his neediness.

Danny Zuker ✓
@DannyZuker

You see @realDonaldTrump often on April 1st people will say one thing and mean the opposite, so when I say you're not a terrible person...

1:31 AM – 6 Apr 2014

16 Retweets **98** Likes

Danny Zuker ✓
@DannyZuker

So @realDonaldTrump maybe rethink this tweet. Hate to see you make a public idiot of yourself. #LOL #SomewhatNice

‹   Tweet   🔍 ✍

Donald J. Trump ✓   +👤
@realDonaldTrump

"@DannyZuker: I may disagree with much of what @realDonaldTrump says, but that doesn't mean I think he's a terrible person. Somewhat nice!

1:42 AM – 6 Apr 2014

16 Retweets **98** Likes

I almost felt bad for him. Almost.

Danny Zuker ✔
@DannyZuker

Suck it, @realDonaldTrump!

1:42 AM – 6 Apr 2014

457 Retweets **1,800** Likes

He has no Emmys. I'm not above gloating.

Epilogue

I like to imagine an alternate timeline where that final tweet is the end of the story. Where twenty years from now, someone mentions my feud and my grandchild asks, "Who's Donald Trump?" And I chuckle and say, "Oh, just some asshole who died penniless in a Reno whore house," and then my daughter reprimands me for cussing in front of the children and we laugh and laugh. I confess to spending an unhealthy amount of time dreaming of this alternate universe.

But you can't pick your universe and, in this one, somehow, Donald J. Trump became President of the United States of America. (It literally hurts me to type that.) At the time of my writing this, he's been in office for about 500 days and I'm afraid that he still hasn't "pivoted." He's still the stunted simpleton who battled me. Only now, he battles the entire world, with the glaring exception of Vladimir Putin. I would suggest the stakes are somewhat higher.

When I set out to put this book together with Paul Slansky I had three goals. In no particular order:

Raise money for organizations whose work is more necessary than ever thanks to Trump and his cronies' mean-spirited policies. A portion of each sale will go directly to these organizations fighting the good fight every day: Planned Parenthood, RAICES (the Refugee and Immigrant Center for Education and Legal Services) and the World Wildlife Fund.

Get the attention and praise from strangers that I never got from my dad.

Put to rest the notion that Trump is secretly some kind of brilliant strategist.

That last one drives me the craziest. To this day I hear pundits speculating, "What is Trump's strategy on (fill in the blank)?" You've read this book. You've lived in this world. Does he seem like a man capable of playing three-dimensional chess? Every action, every tweet, is in service of one thing: protecting the image of Donald J. Trump. Making people believe he is all the things he desperately wishes he was: Respected, Smart, Tough, Rich, Successful and Sexy. He hates the Russian investigation not because he'd be exposed as a traitor but because he'd be exposed as a loser. Every time we take him seriously, and not for the fool he is, he wins and we lose. And that's just #Sad.

About The Authors

When not trolling the leader of the free world, **Danny Zuker** (@DannyZuker) works as a television comedy writer/producer. He's spent the last nine years as one of the executive producers of *Modern Family*, and has worked on many shows including *Evening Shade*, *Roseanne*, *Just Shoot Me*, and so many flops.

Paul Slansky (@slansky) is the author of *The Clothes Have No Emperor: A Chronicle of the American '80s* and five other books that savagely mock the idiots, hypocrites and demagogues who masquerade as our "leaders." In the summer of 2016, he created (and continues to curate) *www.trumpelthinskin.com*, a website dedicated to disrespecting Donald Trump.

Acknowledgments

A list of names of all the family members, friends, and countless others whose shared horror at this grotesque spectacle have helped keep us sane would fill a volume many times the size of this book. One name, though, deserves special mention – Daniel Vallancourt, without whose tireless efforts this book would not exist. Thank you, Dan.

It turns out that the worst among us bring out the best in many of us. The preternatural odiousness of Donald Trump, his family and his staff – and, of course, of the complicit legislative quislings who have, whether actively or passively, enabled his ongoing destruction of America as we've known it – has inspired the most scathingly brilliant writing and art of our lifetimes, along with tens of millions – if not hundreds of millions – of savage social media postings. All of those who have given voice to their disgust, contempt and outrage have our eternal gratitude, as well as the admiration of those who will look back on this time with utter scorn for those who remained silent.

CPSIA information can be obtained
at www.ICGtesting.com
Printed in the USA
LVHW06s0609110918
589679LV00002B/2/P

9 780999 845288